Flies

by Cheryl Coughlan

Consulting Editor: Gail Saunders-Smith, Ph.D.
Consultant: Gary A. Dunn, Director of Education,
Young Entomologists' Society

Pebble Books

an imprint of Capstone Press
Mankato, Minnesota

Pebble Books are published by Capstone Press
818 North Willow Street, Mankato, Minnesota 56001
http://www.capstone-press.com

Library of Congress Cataloging-in-Publication Data
Coughlan, Cheryl.
    Flies/by Cheryl Coughlan.
    p. cm.—(Insects)
    Includes bibliographical references (p. 23) and index.
    Summary: Simple text and photographs present the features and behavior of
flies.
    ISBN 0-7368-0240-1
    1. Flies—Juvenile literature. [1. Flies.] I. Title. II. Series: Insects (Mankato, Minn.)
QL533.2.C68 1999
595.77—dc21   98—55562
                                                                              CIP
                                                                              AC

Note to Parents and Teachers

The Insects series supports national science standards for units on the diversity and unity of life. The series shows that animals have features that help them live in different environments. This book describes and illustrates the parts of flies. The photographs support early readers in understanding the text. The repetition of words and phrases helps early readers learn new words. This book also introduces early readers to subject-specific vocabulary words, which are defined in the Words to Know section. Early readers may need assistance to read some words and to use the Table of Contents, Words to Know, Read More, Internet Sites, and Index/Word List sections of the book.

2

Table of Contents

Flies have two wings.

haltere

Flies have two halteres
that help them fly.

8

Most flies have hair.

Flies have large eyes
made of many lenses.

12

Flies spit on food
to make it soft.

proboscis

Flies use a proboscis
to suck food into
the mouth.

16

Flies have six legs.

18

Flies have sticky feet.

Most flies can walk
upside down.

Words to Know

eye—a body part used for seeing; flies have large compound eyes made of many small lenses; flies can see in nearly all directions at the same time.

halteres—two knobs near flies' wings that help them maintain balance; flies use their halteres to change direction while flying.

proboscis—a long, tube-shaped mouthpart; flies eat by sucking food through a proboscis.

spit—to force saliva out of the mouth; flies spit on food to make it soft; this helps them suck food through the proboscis.

sticky—tending to stay attached; flies have sticky pads on their feet to help them walk upside down.

wing—a movable part of an insect that helps it fly; most winged insects have four wings, but flies have only two.

Read More

Hunt, Joni Phelps. *Insects.* Close-up. Parsippany, N.J.: Silver Burdett Press, 1995.

Sullivan, D. K. *Do Flies Have Eyes?: A Book about Bugs.* Ask Kermit. Racine, Wisc.: Western Publishing, 1995.

Wilkinson, Valerie. *Flies Are Fascinating.* Rookie Read-About Science. Chicago: Children's Press, 1994.

Wilsdon, Christina. *National Audubon Society First Field Guide: Insects.* New York: Scholastic, 1998.

Internet Sites

Flies: The Joys of Sticky Feet
http://www.letsfindout.com/subjects/bug/rfiflyft.html

Flies: Messy Eaters
http://www.letsfindout.com/subjects/bug/rfimouth.html

House Flies
http://bluehen.ags.udel.edu/deces/hyg/hyg-30.htm

Index/Word List

Word Count: 56
Early-Intervention Level: 8

Editorial Credits

Damian C. Koshnick, editor; Timothy Halldin, cover designer; Kimberly Danger, photo researcher

Photo Credits

Bill Johnson, cover
Dwight R. Kuhn, 10
GeoIMAGERY/Joe Warfel, 6, 14
James P. Rowan, 12, 18, 20
Rob Curtis, 4, 16
Robert McCaw, 1
Root Resources/William Glass, 8